CITY OF SALT

ALSO BY GREGORY ORR

POETRY

New and Selected Poems, 1988
We Must Make a Kingdom of It, 1986
The Red House, 1980
Gathering the Bones Together, 1975
Burning the Empty Nests, 1973

CRITICISM

Richer Entanglements: Essays and Notes
        on Poetry and Poems, 1993
Stanley Kunitz: An Introduction to the Poetry, 1985

CITY OF SALT

Gregory Orr

University of Pittsburgh Press
Pittsburgh • London

The publication of this book is supported by grants from the National Endowment for the Arts in Washington, D.C., a Federal agency, and the Pennsylvania Council on the Arts.

Published by the University of Pittsburgh Press, Pittsburgh, Pa. 15260
Manufactured in the United States of America
Printed on acid-free paper
Second printing 1995

Library of Congress Cataloging-in-Publication Data
Orr, Gregory.
City of salt / Gregory Orr
      p.   cm. —(Pitt Poetry Series)
    ISBN 0-8229-3876-6 (cl.).—ISBN 0-8229-5557-1 (pbk.)
    I. Title.   II. Series.
    PS3565.R7C58   1995   94-42339
    811'.54—dc20   CIP
A CIP catalogue record for this book is available from the British Library.
Eurospan, London

The author and publisher wish to acknowledge the following publications in which some of these poems first appeared:

American Poetry Review ("City of Salt," "Elegy for a Child," "The Gray Fox," "Litany," "My Father's Voice," "The Vase," "A Visitor," "Who'd Want to be a Man?"); *Antioch Review* ("After Piero Cosima's *Venus and Sleeping Mars*," "The Hinge"); *Boulevard* ("The Fire Hydrant," "Suspicions"); *Carolina Quarterly*, ("Annunciation"); *Denver Quarterly* ("The Cliff"); *Harvard Magazine* ("A La Mysterieuse"); *Iris* ("The Change"); *Michigan Quarterly Review* ("Scarlet T-shirt: The Lyric Muse"); *Ohio Review* ("I Found a Bird"); *Ontario Review* ("Everything," "House of Childhood," "A Moment"); *Poetry* ("Glukupikron"); *Southern Review* ("The Motorcycle"); *Sycamore Review* ("Lament," "Muse of Midnight"); and *Zone 3* ("The Cherry Orchards").

"The Cliff" and "The Gray Fox" appeared in *The Breadloaf Book of Nature Poetry*.

Paperback cover and section divider art: Josef Sudek. Photograph copyright © by UPM/Decorative Art Museum in Prague, arranged through Takarajima Books, New York, New York.

Book Design: Frank Lehner

For Trisha, Eliza, and Sophia

Contents

III. TALES OUT OF TIME

IV. CITY OF SALT

I. HOUSE OF CHILDHOOD

ORIGIN OF THE MARBLE FOREST

Childhood dotted with bodies.

Let them go, let them
be ghosts.

No, I said,
make them stay, make them stone.

A LITANY

I remember him falling beside me,
the dark stain already seeping across his parka hood.
I remember screaming and running the half mile to our house.
I remember hiding in my room.
I remember that it was hard to breathe
and that I kept the door shut in terror that someone would enter.
I remember pressing my knuckles into my eyes.
I remember looking out the window once
at where an ambulance had backed up
over the lawn to the front door.
I remember someone hung from a tree near the barn
the deer we'd killed just before I shot my brother.
I remember toward evening someone came with soup.
I slurped it down, unable to look up.
In the bowl, among the vegetable chunks,
pale shapes of the alphabet bobbed at random
or lay in the shallow spoon.

A MOMENT

The field where my brother died—
I've walked there since.
Weeds and grasses, some chicory
stalks; no trace of the scene
I still can see: a father
and his sons bent above
a deer they'd shot,
then screams and shouts.

Always I arrive too late
to take the rifle
from the boy I was,
too late to warn him
of what he can't imagine:
how quickly people vanish;
how one moment you're standing
shoulder to shoulder,
the next you're alone in a field.

HAITI, 1961

—from the Hôpital Albert Schweitzer

My mother writes her dearest friend:
"We had to leave; we had to go away
and try again in another place.
And the need here is appalling—
how poor these people are!"

There's evil in this country. I blame
the government: Papa Doc who glowers
like an owl from oval portraits
on the postage stamps, who arms
the goons who stop our car
in every town.

"On Jim's day off we rented horses,
started up a path. It got so narrow
we couldn't turn back—deep ravines
on either side. We had to trek
to the top of the mountain,
come back by another path."

Next week, she's dead at thirty-six.
When the rains come, the roar
on the tin roof
so loud that shouting a foot apart
you can't be heard.

HOUSE OF CHILDHOOD

From her sewing nook, nothing finished
will ever emerge. Bolts of cloth,
enough for a small shop;
and the tall green Singer
always between her and her kids:
small suitors sprawled
on the floor, bought off
with boxes of unmatched buttons
they study as if they were foreign coins.

Look at this one—large and black
and carved with an anchor:
from the navy, from the war
he left her for, who leaves her now
each dawn with his doctor's bag
and won't return till way past dark.
Isn't he still at sea, rising
and falling to his secret rhythm
of amphetamine and sleeping pills?
Has anyone seen him in years?

Telemachus, your father's gone,
your mother's cold and distant.
You must hurry and grow up!
You must leave this house
where those from whom you
wanted love live out their lives.

EVERYTHING

—for my mother

Is this all life is then—
only the shallow breaths
I watch you struggle for?
That gasp right now—
if it was water
it would be such a small glass.

And I could lift your head
from the hospital pillow
and help you sip it
to comfort your parched
throat
into the ease of sleep.

Your agony makes no
sense when air
is everywhere, filling
this room where you lie
dying, where we move
as if in a trance, as if
everything were under water.

The Citadel

—Cap Haitien, Haiti, 1961

Though it's only midmorning, it's already a hundred degrees as you climb the four miles of switchback. Near the top, there's a cannon just off the path; then you emerge onto the jungle peak where the huge fort looms above you with the swoop of a battleship's prow.

And now you've arrived below the outer walls, now you enter by the single gate and the guide conducts you up along the ramparts lined with giant bronze cannon (your mother and father still with you, your brothers and sister not yet withdrawn into their separate griefs and destinies).

Then he leads you down to a storeroom piled high with rusted cannonballs. It's cool here; there's a breeze flickering the cupped flame of his candle—no windows anywhere, but a ventilation system, shafts along the wall dug down into the mountain. And then he lifts a twenty-pound cannonball and heaves it into the dark slot of the shaft. You hear it bounce with a loud, sharp "bock" off one wall, then begin to ricochet; longer seconds pass, then the same sound softened by distance, then again. You stand there in a dark lit only by the guide's candle, straining to hear the sounds that are fainter and then fainter still, but never stop.

In the House of Orphans

Their father gone since dawn,
the four of them sit at breakfast.
The oldest smokes. They eat
their toast and jam. Soon
the school bus will take them
from this dark house; then,
in the afternoon,
it will bring them back again.

A Dark Night

How I long to pull the old man in;
he's thrashing out there in the water,
he's drunk and can't swim.

Then again, maybe it's a dog
and he'll claw and bite me
as I lean from the small boat
to haul him up.

           The splashing
so near and those sounds—
are they growls
or a human's choked sobs?
How dark it is; how far I am from shore.

ELEGY

Here are consoling pieties
like a tightly packed
warehouse
of mortuary statues
through which you
must elbow a path.

Here are sparrows
on a porch
sorting sand from seed
with their beaks.

Here's the hour
that has forgotten
the minute
though the minnow
remembers the stream.

Here are the roots
in one world
and the blossom
in the other.

II. WHO'D WANT

WHO'D WANT TO BE A MAN?

With his heart
a black sack
in which a small
animal's trapped.

With his grief
like a knot
tied at birth,
balled up and hard.

With his rage
that smashes the ten
thousand things
without blinking.

With his mind
like a tree on a cliff—
its roots, fists
clutching stone.

With his longing
that's a dry well
and where is the rain?

THE DOOR

A little wall of wood that gives,
that, ajar, yields to a nudge
and reveals what?
                            Everything
that had been concealed behind it,
just like love.
                            No, I mean
like the resistance to love,
the dust on the dark table
that wants to stay there,
or the table itself trembling
like a horse's flank as your hand
slides its smooth length.

And the door, on its hinges, remembers
your palm pressed firm and flat,
remembers you moving into the room beyond,
no phantom but a living thing.

THE VASE

Boredom and terror, and the older
I get the more terror arrives
dressed as boredom, wearing
the same clothes I wear to work
each day.

        Returning home, I empty
my pockets into a large vase
in the hall: bits of lint, scraps
of paper, loose change, a piece of string.

The vase is taller than I am,
blazoned with white chrysanthemums
and green, exotic birds in flight.

NIGHT JOURNEY

I leave the house,
its low room
where my wife sits
knitting beside
a corpse in a coffin.

Out here, bones
of sumac rattle.
Out here, moonlight
on blue snow
crusted thick
and slippery so
I walk slow
and with my arms out.

Just because my shadow
has ragged wings
that doesn't mean
there's another world.

Just because the empty
sparrow's nest
in the thornbush
bursts into flame.

THE MOTORCYCLE

Twenty years ago, zipping
the black jacket tight
at waist and wrists
I entered my own death
like walking down steps
into a dark pool at night;
or I heard oceans
as I lowered the white shell
of the helmet over my head.

Twisted bits of junk
rusting in a ditch—
that's what the motorcycle
should be by now,
yet I see it so clearly:

wheels removed, set on blocks
at the shadowy back of a garage,
black carapace thick
with oily dust:
                        locust
that's dug its way up,
split open to release a creature
that dries its wings,
prepares its shrill cry.

A La Mysterieuse

Only in books I knew you
or in dreams where,
elusive, you were the bit
of dress that disappeared
in the city filled with light
which I knew and did not
know, its streets
constantly shifting.
                    Nothing
prepared me to meet you,
to round a corner
and find you
whom Heraclitus worshipped,
dipping his hand
in the river of your hair,
letting the current
take it
to the small of your back.

MUSE OF MIDNIGHT

In the street, stars collide,
parts of their bodies
breaking off
like chunks of salt.

Still, you hold her,
you're not letting go.
She's the bright-colored
bird with real feathers
and a toy heart, or
toy feathers and a real
heart.

        When all this started
you were lying on a couch.
Now you rise
through the ceiling,
now you're roiled in a cloud,
now you're rain falling
toward its target: a room in flames.

TRISTAN AND ISEULT

Tristan and Iseult had nothing
on me—shown a bonfire
I'd hop aboard
as gladly as if
it were an ice floe
drifting north,
and as fat dripped
from my bones
I'd be wrapping up
in aurora borealis
just to keep warm.

Fire and ice—
at that intensity
the distinction's lost.

Love or hate—who
can say
when the need's that deep?

On dark nights I'd
reach up toward her face—
sometimes it was the moon,
sometimes a radiant
ax blade
descending to kiss my wrists.

THE HINGE

On it the whole world turns
if the world is a door,
and if the world is not a door
how to explain that movement
seen in the butterfly's
stiff wings
as it flutters
on a purple bush,
or the arms of lovers
thrown open
on their equally precise
pivots.
      And the hinge
screams as it yields
though no one's there,
though it's only the breeze.

The Fire Hydrant

Little stump of a thing stuck on the curb of my street: dull as bark, with no leaves or branches. For you, the truth is rust, although here and there a brass fitting may last forever—like those perfect teeth the skeleton flosses on the poster in my dentist's office. And I know he means well, my conscientious little dentist whom I hate, who's trying to frighten me awake before it's too late.

He's like that hydrant I mock and pity. When flames break out in my house, he's the small man at the back of the crowd gushing his lifeblood through the open valves of his heart, selflessly weeping for all he's worth.

And where am I? My whole house is burning down and all I do is stand on the lawn and gaze at the fire—that beautiful woman leaping from the window in her bright red dress.

THE CLIFF

Below me treetops and a crow
making its slow progress.
The green canopy's no sea
or net, but that absolute—
thin veil between
the living and the dead.

Confusion of thickets behind me;
before me, open space.

From time to time returning
to this granite ledge
where I measure my life
by refusals, here
where measuring starts,
less than a step from the edge.

THE GRAY FOX

Someone I know is dying at seventeen.
When he visited last Thanksgiving
he wore with an adolescent's joy
the black leather jacket I lent him.

Around us spring happens: a crocus
among the gravestones, plum blossoms
that open in a single night.

Already ivy twines the fence wire
and last year's path through the field
vanishes in the thick green of new grass.

It would be good to be the gray fox
that trots to pond's edge, spots me
and stops. All winter he's hunted here,
undisturbed, and now he watches me
watch him, ten yards away, unafraid.

SELF-PORTRAIT AT TWENTY

I stood inside myself
like a dead tree or a tower.
I pulled the rope
of braided hair
and high above me
a bell of leaves tolled.

Because my hand
stabbed its brother,
I said: make it stone.

Because my tongue
spoke harshly, I said:
make it dust.

         And yet
it was not death, but
her body in its green dress
I longed for. That's why
I stood for days in the field
until the grass turned black
and the rain came.

LOOKING BACK

Marble pillars
of palace
or temple—
so what?
I've seen them
tumbled by vines.

And our beautiful
bodies—
how long
will they last?

Shallow valley
where we
lay down,
crushing a circle
in tall grass.

Above it
our ghosts
drifted
in rowboats
among low clouds,
letting down
lines
of sunlight with
tiny golden hooks.

LAMENT

I thought of you
as I drove past
the girl kneeling
on the verge
by her upside-down
bicycle.

      I know
she was only
fixing the chain
but for one moment
I saw her playing
a round harp
(and I thought of you
as I drove past).

There on the highway's
edge where gusts
from passing cars
whipped the grass
like wind off the sea,
she was kneeling,
her arms moving
among the metal spokes
plucking from them
a music lost
in the louder
impersonal sound
of traffic (and I thought
of you
as I drove past).

The girl kneeling
on the verge,

adjusting the loop
of metal links
that would propel her
into the future,
but also playing
(and I thought of you
as I drove past)
a round harp
on a desolate coast.

III. Tales Out of Time

AFTER PIERO COSIMA'S
VENUS AND SLEEPING MARS

Naked on the ground,
they both recline
in opposite directions.
The god's asleep,
the goddess lies awake,
smiling,
propped on an elbow,
her tilted face
held in her open palm.

In the background
wolves skulk
to their lairs,
tails close-curled
like soldiers
quitting a field
with banners furled;
as if the thrust
of this scene
is not the adage
that lust disrupts
but something
about its aftermath:
how the world's made safe
for one more day:
Venus's hares hopping about
Mars's discarded armor.

BETRAYALS/HADES, EURYDICE, ORPHEUS

She stood before his throne,
her body so beautiful
it made the old king wince.

And we ghosts, gray husks,
gathered close as if
to warm ourselves at embers.

Then *he* entered, his boots
like thunder echoing
in that dark, silent hall.

And what had he brought?
Songs of anguish and desire—
all she had gladly forgot.

His words about the world
were meant to lure her back,
to hurt her into memory.

And they worked. I watched
her brow furrow,
her placid face lose all repose.

I thought we'd lost her then
until our sly king
whispered in the singer's ear:

"Take her. She's yours.
And trust her if you dare,
but be alert.

Do not turn your back on her."

INVESTIGATION

This much is known:
the thread you never
let go of
guided you back.
And when you emerged,
years later, light
hurt your eyes.
Blood on your rusted
blade was dry.

But what happened
in the labyrinth?
In deepest dark
you grappled,
felt its breath
on your face,
stabbed,
and fled.

        A monster?
Wouldn't *anything*
cry like that,
pierced to the heart?

The Change

—for a former student

Circe was said to do that,
change men into the beasts
they most resembled.
But this is different:
a young woman who's
the skittish pony
that was her childhood's
only consolation:
                    fearful,
tensed at a touch,
balking at twig snaps,
terror in the eyes
and the mind racing.

Horror she can't name;
not Circe, but her father.

PENELOPE/THE WHITE DOOR

Sometimes when I'm beyond hope
and come here for refuge,
when I've just entered
this dark room where the loom
leans against the far wall
and the white cloth glows
like an open door,
I see her silhouetted against it,
the goddess of thresholds,
she who greets by turning away,
whose face gazes out
at the infinite and unknown
as if she's only pausing
in this moment
before she steps through
into the dazzling light of the next.

IN THE ART MUSEUM

To the guard I'm probably only another oaf from the sticks, one of those people he's paid to intimidate. He can see the dried cow dung still clinging to my shoes.

But doesn't that Dutch barnyard scene belong to me? The old woman herding geese with a willow switch; that tiny figure lugging a milk yoke? And the way his arms steady it, as if he were martyred to a cross: a life of sacrifice that leaves no trace.

No trace at all except this canvas daubed with paint in this huge marble hall where I stand in a shaft of light, under the guard's scowl, my hat clasped behind my back and absently tapping my pants so that the dust that rises from them turns to gold in the air.

SUSPICIONS

If you wander in the market
you'll find little signs
of infiltration—a certain crudeness
in the carving of a ladle
or a mask whose features
differ subtly from the temple god's.
I'm not saying the trader
is himself a barbarian;
it's more elusive than that.
Maybe he merely passed
some time among them, yet
his wares have changed
the way a lake in sun is not
the same lake when a cloud comes
or the way your wife smells
different after a party
when she's talked with other men.

ANNUNCIATION

In Simone Martini's *Annunciation*
an angel kneels on parquet
and mouths golden Greek letters
that rise in a line
toward the Virgin's ear.

Despite his halo and earnest
gaze, the olive bough he holds,
she leans away,
regards him with a sideways
skeptical look.

                    And isn't that
us: me unreeling
an implausible line,
you doubting it completely
yet needing to believe
something even more unlikely,
that a man could be an angel.

GLUKUPIKRON

—to Sappho

Word you created
which we translate
bittersweet
         thereby
reversing the terms
as if we thought pain
came first
and pleasure only later;
for you maybe joy
was initial,
to be followed
by harsh disappointment.

Yet in the word itself
the two fuse,
and in the condition
it refers to
they mingle,
indistinguishable,
not to be separated
by any force.

It was
your word for love.

Aubade

Up and down the street the sound
of coffins closing.
No, it's only
car doors slamming,
people off to work.

Behold the lilies,
Jesus said, they
neither toil nor spin
yet Solomon
in all his glory
was not
arrayed as them.

Perhaps he meant
some other world.
Here, lawns are shorn
and Samson's trapped
in the daily round:
chained to the mill,
he grinds his enemies' corn.

SCARLET T-SHIRT: THE LYRIC MUSE

I know I'm vulgar, but so
was noble Catullus;
nor does Latin lend
his lines a dignity
my Anglo-Saxon lacks.

And what about Sappho?
Didn't her poems
full of moans
teach us that passion
is the only song that lasts?

▼

Let her sister muses
keep their curves
chastely garbed,
their tresses bound up
in formal buns.
Hell, let them dress
in prose like Joseph's
many-colored coat,
a fitting emblem
of the world's
variety and splendor.

But she must go
naked, or
in something intense
and crude
like this scarlet
T-shirt a poet
gave me years ago:
too loud for him,
just right for me.

▼

So what if it's faded
and tattered past
all mending?
Tonight my wife
pulls it on
over her beautiful shoulders
to wear to bed.

▼

Ten years ago
the fabric was intact,
its hue bright
as a macaw's plumes.
Now it's a memento
mori peekaboo;
through its erotic,
oracular gaps
I glimpse her ribs,
swell of a breast:
what breaks the heart
and will not let it rest.

IV. City of Salt

FULL MOON

Projector's beam.
                    Wasn't it
only yesterday I stood
on my seat and reached up
to cast shadows on the blank screen?

THE GIFT

—for my daughter

Scissors, glue, clumsy
fingers—crude tools
I've used to make
this cardboard bird
I've painted bright
unlikely colors
and hung by a string
above your crib.

▼

In last night's dream
you were grown
and I was old
and in the backyard
digging a deep hole.
You stood above me
shining a light
where I shoveled down
through all my life.

▼

In an ancient book,
Bede wrote
how a sparrow flew
from dark through
a lighted meadhall
into dark again.

▼

Tiny wings of your lungs—
each beat a breath.

FATHER'S SONG

Yesterday, against admonishment,
my daughter balanced on the couch back,
fell, and cut her mouth.

Because I saw it happen I knew
she was not hurt, and yet
a child's blood's so red
it stops a father's heart.

My daughter cried her tears;
I held some ice
against her lip.
That was the end of it.

Round and round; bow and kiss.
I try to teach her caution;
she tries to teach me risk.

THE SEARCH

All night you search for them
in the dark house.
How is it they have vanished?
Where could they go?
Empty rooms proliferate;
outside doors are locked.
The car parked in the driveway
is covered with snow.
Their bed is cold as though
no one had warmed it
in a thousand years.

CARTOONS

My wife rises every few hours to nurse our infant, so these mornings I get up with our three year old while she sleeps a little longer. I make our daughter breakfast then sit her in front of the TV to watch *Sesame Street*. After that, I have twenty minutes or so to sip coffee and browse some book in the morning quiet.

But today is Sunday and *Sesame Street* isn't on yet, so I sit with my daughter on the couch, trying to find something that interests her on the eight channels we get. It's animated cartoons she likes best and when we come upon one as I flip through, she says, "Stop! This one."

It's set in ancient Phoenicia—a little girl in a hut; her legs were hurt somehow, so she's crippled. Her mother's distraught and doesn't know what to do, but a neighbor says, "I understand that Jesus can work miracles and he's nearby. Shall I ask him to come?" The mother answers, "But he's a Jew, and I am a Phoenician—why would he help me?" In her despair, she decides to seek him out anyway.

My daughter is totally caught up and wants to keep watching—no doubt she identifies with the little girl who lies on her cot and tries to be brave. But there's something I don't like about this story or about how raptly my daughter watches it. So, despite her cries and complaints, I start searching the channels again.

The only other cartoon I can find is *Masters of the Universe*—violent science fiction in which human figures constantly metamorphose into war machines in order to fight other machines or blue-skinned extraterrestrial demons. "This one!" my daughter shouts with great authority.

Giving up, I leave it on and go upstairs. The book I pull down is Plato's *Republic*. I have some vague idea of locating his definition of the lyric poem, but instead what I find in the first minutes of leafing through is Socrates' argument for censorship in education. He's especially angry at the poets for telling stories that "misrepresent the nature of gods and heroes." After all, he reasons, children are totally determined by what they're exposed to: "any impression we choose to make leaves a permanent mark."

God help me if that's true. But Plato's wrong if he believes my daughter's mind is only clay or wax. She was born intense and decisive, no one made her that way. Thirty seconds out of the womb, red-faced and squirming on her mother's belly, you could tell by her look she had strong views.

Maybe she got her father's fierceness as some code on her chromosomes along with his deep-set eyes. If so, at least she got her mother's kindness as well. I'm mulling all this over as I sip my coffee, when I hear a knock at the door. A couple: a black man in his twenties in a gray suit and an older white woman in a prim dress and horn-rimmed glasses. They both hold bibles over their hearts. "Good morning," she says, "I wonder if we might talk to you about Jesus." Almost without thinking, I say, "No, that's not what interests me." "Well then, perhaps we could just share a Bible thought with you." "No," I say, closing the door.

I watch them turn and go back down the walk through the early morning fog that is rarely so thick here in Virginia. I could call them back, but instead I'm thinking about my tiny grandmother who lived alone on the coast of Maine where such thick fogs are common.

She was my mother's mother—the only true believer I ever knew— a bedrock Christian and stalwart supporter of the John Birch Society. The God who worked for her had violent and absolute opinions. From my earliest childhood visits, she filled me with fear, and as I grew that fear turned to something deeper and more harsh than distaste; a feeling that even today makes me ashamed.

By now my coffee's cold and Plato's perfect society, from which I and all my colleagues are banished for our lies and lack of faith, seems not worth returning to. Since I must be exiled, I might as well go downstairs and sit with my daughter. Whether she's soft clay or not, she's what I've got, what I've begotten. She bears her scars and gifts into America's future. And since I'm the one who refused the cartoon of compassionate healing, the least I can do is share with her what's left, what even now the TV's crescendo of sound announces: a last battle in which the heroes have become machines that blow apart all the evil robots with powerful beams of light.

I Found a Bird

1

In the old story
the children in the forest
were frightened
until one brave boy
entered the wolf's huge
mouth and came back
holding in his hands
Satan's heart.

2. Some Sentences My Daughter Eliza Wrote

I found a bird.
It is night.
I am small.
I am happy now.
The lamp is lit.

3

Sophie wants the light on
when she sleeps.
She wants the door closed.

Her sister wakes at six
and climbs into our bed
to sleep again.

4

The wolf wasn't evil.
It wasn't even a wolf
but an old man

into whose side
Satan thrust his heart
so that the man
changed into a wolf.

5

When I wake in the night
I feel small, feel
frightened of all
the world contains.
I turn on the lamp.
I sit up in bed,
my heart heavy.

6

Satan was angry
about the singing.
The boy had taught
the children to walk
in the forest, singing.

7

Wasn't I that brave boy
once, who am now almost
an old man, and frightened?

CLEAR NIGHT

Trudging new snow to the shed,
entering its dark.
Fresh, unsplit logs
cover the back wall,
make a pattern like cells
in a wintering hive.

And the sap smell, too,
dense as the waxy odor of combs.
Breathing it in so deeply
I need to close my eyes.

Out again into the no-smell
of cold air. The wood,
bundled in its carryall,
pulls my arm one way,
I lean the other.
Dogs bark in a far yard.

Looking out over the wide world:
field after white field,
then the wooded mountain
where lights shine:
neighbors, other lives.

THE PATH

It doesn't go anywhere;
bluestone and slate
from a pile I found out back
and plopped down on the grass
in a ragged line
below the garden slope.

How proud I was,
believing it was done.

A year's passed and now
all I see is hazard:
cracks between uneven stones
where my daughters
will trip
and hurt themselves.

So I kneel here,
trowel in hand, digging
the whole thing up
to lay it flat.

As I lift each stone
I think of those I loved
now dead and buried deep,
and how this too is both
lament and celebration,
a father's dream
of his daughters running
a path he made.

MY FATHER'S VOICE

Even as I rage, I see my daughter
wince and cringe
as I did too, ages ago,
as if braced
against sudden wind,
blinking quickly, then her face
going blank as a mask
while in the heart a green bush
weathers the shaping blast.

ELEGY

1. A GRAVE RUBBING

You place the paper against
an old slab of New England
granite. Moving the flat
stick of charcoal back
and forth in smooth strokes
as though it were a broom
and you were sweeping
dead leaves from a porch.

A winged skull emerges,
then a scrap of scripture,
dates and a name.

2. LIFE MASK

That cast of Keats's face
I keep on my shelf—
precise shape, all lines
and features, round
of his chin, brow-slope,
his eyelids closed
not in death, but
against wet plaster
his friend placed there
one afternoon
a hundred and seventy
years ago.
                A face
not ravaged by illness
but here in youthful health,

this generous man
whose mouth made beautiful sounds,
whose flesh is nothing now.

3. CHILD'S GAME

What I want is
to preserve my friend—
the outline of his face,
every mortal wrinkle,
against that moment
when the hospital sheet
is pulled up over his face
like white paper, like
the child's game
where paper covers rock
as snow might blanket
a graveyard, covering
all the stones, making
the landscape smooth and blank.

THE CHERRY ORCHARDS

—Summer, 1960

At dawn the dew was cold and thick
in the high grass between the rows
as each in turn
dropped from the flatbed truck
and waded toward his chosen trees.

But what was I doing there,
not yet fourteen, and so
scrawny I couldn't lift
my long oak ladder, much less
place it firmly.

                Every half hour
a different picker appeared
below me, shouted "Get down,"
then grabbed the rungs and flung it
without a wasted motion
among the unpicked branches
where the bright fruit shone.

When your life's worth twenty cents
a bucket, no time to fool around,
and so, before I could blurt
a word of thanks, each
anonymous body vanished
among the leaves, reclaiming
its place in a jocular chorus
which rose all day above the trees.

Under Pressure

It had to do with yellow poplar leaves
that fell in windy rain last night
and how the path through the woods
(the shortcut I walk to work)
was partly obscured;
I only sensed its outline,
a shallow depression
no deeper than a wordless sigh
or the dent above a child's grave.

If you were there I would have tried
to tell you about it, you
who believe the world
is real and calls us
with a voice stronger than sorrow.

I listed my blessings: all those
I love who hold me here.
I looked up at the thick
interlacing of branches above my head
and saw, high up, the bright blue
of air I might breathe, air I could swim to.

Three Small Songs

1

A shaft of wind
on the lake
makes a path
across the water.

This world is real
and beautiful;
we're here
and then we're gone.

2

When I was young
and my mother died
I was afraid
if I started to cry
I'd never stop.

3

Pungent smell of deep grass
at dusk as I lay
in hide and seek,
my small heart beating
against the dark earth . . .

THE CITY OF SALT

In the sun-drenched
city of salt
where the window boxes
are little coffins
full of red geraniums,
flower
that offers up
earth's smell of death
like water
from a deep well.

In that city of salt
where my mother walks
with a basket
over one arm—
she's off to market,
she's going to buy
all those things
she forgot to give us
when she was alive.

In that city of salt
the sun never sets,
the rooms of her apartment
fill up
with vegetables:
the purple globes
of eggplant, asparagus
like the blunt bolts
a crossbow fires,
and peppers convoluted
as the heart
and sweet to taste.

Photo: Trisha Orr

Gregory Orr ————————

lives with his wife, the painter Trisha Orr, and his two daughters in Charlottesville, Virginia. He is professor of English and director of the M.F.A. program at the University of Virginia and poetry editor of the *Virginia Quarterly Review*. The recipient of a Guggenheim fellowship and two National Endowment for the Arts fellowships in poetry, he is the author of five previous collections of poetry and two critical works.

PITT POETRY SERIES

Ed Ochester, General Editor

Made in the USA
Middletown, DE
18 June 2020